Gallery Books
Editor Peter Fallon

THE IMPORTANT THINGS

Audrey Molloy

THE IMPORTANT THINGS

Gallery Books

The Important Things
is first published
simultaneously in paperback
and in a clothbound edition
on 24 June 2021.

The Gallery Press
Loughcrew
Oldcastle
County Meath
Ireland

www.gallerypress.com

ISBN 978 1 91133 802 4 *paperback*
     978 1 91133 803 1 *clothbound*

A CIP catalogue record for this book
is available from the British Library.

The Important Things receives financial assistance
from the Arts Council.

Contents

PART ONE

The Apprentice *page* 13
A Brief History of Smoking 14
Envy Is a Day Lily 16
How I Knew It Was a Dream 17
What We Learned at Loreto 18
Elegy for a Limb 19
Arc of a Love Story 20
Contranyms of Loss, or The Husband's Tale 22
Ghost Gum 23
The Courser's Tale 24
On Reaching 45 the Poet Realizes She Is Only 23 25
The Ologist's Ego, Conquered 26
Mother Creature 28
Chrysalis 30
Naming the First-born 31
My Son at Bedtime 32
Motel Ghosts 33
The Irish for Yes 34
Grey Man 36
Lockdown Boogie 37
The Important Things 38
Skin Symphony 40
A Gradual Eden 42
Sold a Pup 44
Forty-four 45
Poaching Stone Fruit on the Long Weekend 46
What I Learned from the Dentist 47
Curracloe Revisited 51
Unfinished 54
Anna Karenina Smiles as She Steps off the Platform 55

PART TWO

Charmed 59
Flowering Cherry 60

Debutante Dress 61
Like Double Denim 62
Mother, I Am Your Mother Now 64
Uprooted 65
His Hybrid Tea Roses 66
She Loved 67
The Space Between 68
Running Out 69
Going Home 71
Confetti 72
False Memory 73
Pink for a Boy 74
Salt Rain, Wexford 76

Notes 78
Acknowledgements 79

in memory of my mother, Iris

PART ONE

I knew
If I looked too closely they would turn to dust.
As I would, dreaming, if I couldn't reach you,
Solid, asleep in this inn we've carefully built
Of seasoned faith and uncorrupted trust.
— Anne Stevenson ('The Inn')

The Apprentice

She said that we must always wet our lips,
    code for another kind of pleasing.

We were playing a game called Musical Wives
    and she was ahead. We sat in our bias-cut slips,

sipping vermouth in bare feet and lipstick,
    and she told me his genitals looked different

when lying on his side, like the Tsar Pushka cannon
    she saw in the Kremlin, with its half-cocked shaft

and squat wheels. It looks small but feels big, she said,
    like a tooth when your tongue runs along it.

She taught me all her tricks: the royal pudendum,
    presented on a velvet pillow.

We were folding origami butterflies,
    placing them in rows in a shallow drawer.

She told me that it was the other kind of I love you,
    that they *would* marry. As they hurtled forward

in their tin can, trailing a string of cars behind them,
    the air was filled with tiny paper wings.

A Brief History of Smoking

I blame Madonna. My fingerless gloves got me busted. Mother, always the fashionista, tried them on, held them to her cheek, blanched at the whiff of stale smoke and searched my room. The contraband, a pack of *Drum* (Milde Shag), was on my person as I followed her around, but she found it in the pocket of my blazer and burnt it in the Aga.

— ⁓ —

I'd dreamt of *Gauloises*, but that summer we smoked *Lucky Strikes*, lakeside in the Alps near Gap. We were tanned, unaware of our taste in their mouths — the white-teeth boys who offered a light from brass Zippos. Delphine and I swam the lake to escape, walked back on virgin feet, laughing at nothing, bumming a smoke on the way, and who wouldn't give us one?

— ⁓ —

A pool of denim and velvet on the floor between bed and door; sending a taxi for smokes at 3 a.m. — all those things we don't do now, like cigarettes after sex — crackle as leaf becomes ash, sheets of smoke suspended, uplit by a candle in a Mateus Rosé bottle. On the nightstand, like a carriage clock, *Dunhill*'s claret-and-gold pack; alas, now gone, replaced with images that would put you off coming.

— ⁓ —

Lighting up in the fire escape: me, filing clerk, and hot CEO who tells me I should wear red to work more often — you could back then. And the switch to *Silk Cut Ultra*, when you realize addiction is not strictly chemical. I mean, how much nicotine is really in those things? Fourteen years post-quitting, the gaps — still there, after dessert, or

making love, or when news comes on the phone that someone's died.

⌐

The first time you have a panic attack you have no idea
what's happening, only that you cannot read a simple
instruction in English — how to call home from a public
phone in an unfamiliar city. There are only nonsense words,
and lungs that won't fill. Two good pulls on a *Rothmans*
would've shit all over the Xanax they prescribed, but that
only occurred to me years later.

⌐

They tell me I still have the smoker's personality, whatever
that means: *extroverted, tense, impulsive, neurotic, sensation-
seeking* — this last I love: *the search for new, complex, intense
experiences, and the predisposition to take risks in order to do
so, including radical sports, criminal activities, risky sexual
behaviour, alcoholism, use of illicit drugs, gambling.* Well,
maybe I have, and maybe I haven't.

⌐

And now we live to a hundred, nothing left to spare us
from days spent lap-rugged in a wheelchair, staring through
glass at pariahs huddled outside cafés and bars. (*Viva!*
Vivienne Westwood, at the ball, pack of *Marlboro* tucked
up the puff sleeve of her gown.) Can it be that hard to
create a smoke that might grant years of calm and, one
unexpected night, assassinate us in our sleep?

Envy Is a Day Lily

At the end of the street
behind the supermarket
where pretty houses peter out,
there's yours.

Broadleaf weeds
outside the torn fly-screen
where a Cavalier King Charles
eyes you, head to one side.

You can't answer his question,
but know this: someone
once looked upon your life
and wished it were theirs.

How I Knew It Was a Dream

The day was strange from the start.
Small things, like the way the grass
leaned towards the dying moon

or the air lifted the table linen.
The eggs, when rapped lightly on the bowl,
rapped back, and this went on, back

and forth, until I tucked
them in the warm cleft of my breast,
where they sang like happy kettles.

The solemn badger in the hallway
held my Barbour coat as I slipped it on.
A strange day, I tell you.

People were talking in the street
and on the train, heads thrown back
to laugh at nothing. No one wore a mask.

I accepted all this as a marvellous
run of coincidence. That is until
I saw you waving from your car.

I looked around but I was alone,
unmistakable in my velvet cloche,
quilted coat and button-sided boots,

and you, beaming like a man who's spied
a special friend he hasn't seen for years,
not the woman who was once his wife.

What We Learned at Loreto

Nothing useful, like how to apply fake tan
with a sports sock for an even finish
or the way to separate mascara-clotted
eyelashes with the stem of your earring.
Some simple rules would have been handy:
short hem or low-cut — but never together,
and how to keep *a bit of mystery*.
Instead, lists of dates, battles, treaties.
My overnight bag rolls on the back seat
where I threw it before leaving.
All that's keeping me from swift death by lamp-post
is the dashboard clock churning up dates:
Ten fourteen, the Battle of Clontarf.
Eleven eleven, the Synod of Rathbreasail.
Twelve fifteen, the Magna Carta.

Elegy for a Limb

I'd forgotten how he takes his tea.
You'd think fourteen years would leave
an imprint as detailed as the fossil filaments
of a feather; the contours of his hands,
the half-moons of his fingernails.
Fingers are square, the jeweller said,
not round, so he made a four-sided ring,
white gold with a sapphire.
The children said he lost it in the sea.

No milk, his hand blocks the cup.
Say hello to your mother from me, I want to say —
leaving your in-laws, almost as hard
as the rest of it; wounds that bleed for years,
amputations — missing fingers that still
twitch and drum, rub the edge of garments,
lost toes that tip you over in their absence,
loosen your grip on things.

That Christmas after the split
we spent the day together as though
nothing had happened;
their faces solemn on the screen after lunch,
Granny, older somehow, and the brother —
the gift of a brother in a family of sisters —
and the others, unable to smile
at the sight of the woman who left him,
even though there I was
with the children in their Kennedy clothes
and the carcass of a bird
on the cherry-wood dining table
I would leave behind that evening
and never see again.

Arc of a Love Story

15°

When — after the first time we made love — I could hear Puccini
    for days, rising in cafés, shops, tear ducts

30°

when you told me, later, propped on your elbow in the half-
    light, that you never date tall women

45°

when — pretending to read inflight magazines on takeoff,
    forearms just touching — we understood the term *frisson*

60°

when your mouth arched, so proud, in our wedding photo,
    like the silk slipper at the hem of my gown

75°

when they let us take her home, that newly washed day
    in May, a comma tucked in a blanket

90°

when we teetered at the summit, weightless, wondering why
    intimacy was forgotten before children wore us down

105°

when I realized our tin anniversary would never clear
    the horizon, and relinquished every artefact in the house

120°

when I stared at the maps of our home counties, spanning
    an island, until a fissure triggered an avalanche in my chest

135°

when the doorway framed you, the day our dog died, my ribs
    decompressing from your hug

150°
when my heart slid hard against those same ribs as my key
   wouldn't turn in the hall door we'd painted winter white

165°
when *Tosca* still eddies in my tear ducts, though now I can
   listen to most other things dry-eyed

180°
when platinum light reminds me that we shared
   the same moon once, if only for a while.

Contranyms of Loss, or The Husband's Tale

Where once we were joined leaves no scar on me.
Leaves fall from the oak not to hurt the tree
        but to leave a blood-trace confetti
of having left in half-light.

Our colours were fast, no, implacable!
Steadfast as the Dog Star that sparkles
        and dies as fast as man bleeds his life away,
fasting. Without light

beauty turns. The cleft lips of hares know this:
that which cleaves our minds also petrifies,
        cleaving to the known. When you go to him
cleave my soul. Take half.

Ghost Gum

Widow-makers — those boughs that plunge
    without warning, crushing all below.
    Yet I know you are not death but grief's balled fist.

For seven years I decompose beneath your weight,
    implore the fungi to molest me with tiny threads
of Jelly Rot or Sulphur Tuft, but they don't listen.

Take my eye, I whisper to the beetle. Her larvae carve
    your heartwood galleries
    for woodlouse and millipede, but she ignores me.

Acids and mandibles shape your starch and lignins
    to a cross I hunch beneath.
    (Crucifixion: not to kill you, but prolong the pain.)

I find, one day, that I can take a lungful of air,
    push it out through perished chords to sky.
    It was there all along, yet birdless for a time.

Slowly you compress, a constant weight, smaller by the year.
    I guard you like my once-life.
    You are all I have now, instead.

Two thousand degrees of the heart's furnace will spring
    your carbon bonds, form the crystal lattice
of this stone I carry on my index finger,

signalling like a firefly in the forest, *over here!*
    I cannot say that I have nothing
    as long as there exists this one pure, shining thing.

The Courser's Tale

The weight of a small boulder is similar
    to that of a dead dog. I have carried both.

You would think the boulder the heavier,
    but you would be wrong, even for a whippet.

It depends on how much you loved the dog
    but this is not important in the end;

what matters is how much the dog loved you.
    How simple life is for lurcher or Saluki —

find a voice, a scent, and dedicate your life to both.
    Finding purpose, harder for a man:

first, cut out your heart and place it
    in the aviary you have fashioned from the rib-

cage of an owl, then carry it, draped in hessian —
    for the heart used to darkness startles easily —

to the lichen-orange rocks that hide the source
    of your blood and release it.

Let it circle in the water-scented air until,
    lost from sight, it makes its way home,

or slows its beat and drops, light as a finch,
    into the braided stream to be discovered

by a lone explorer, next to a submerged rock,
    or a too-slow hound.

On Reaching 45 the Poet Realizes She Is Only 23

It happened quite by accident, snipping a loose thread from the hem of my corset, the blade nicked my thigh and the tiny wound ran round my leg tin-opener fashion. Not a drop of blood spilt, but my flesh rippled to the ground like a silk stocking freed from its garter on a close afternoon. Beneath, a taut and muscular thigh, covered in a gleaming coat of black hair. I was less shocked than you might imagine, thrilled, in fact, to make this discovery, so I set about freeing the rest of the leg. The ankle was a real sticking point and I had to sit on the floor, prising away flesh with a cheese knife, a box cutter for the tendons, tougher than steel, until there, on the parquetry, lay a coal-black neat and polished hoof. I was quicker with the second leg, applying lessons from the first. Already I could feel a surge of life through my veins, a snort in my nostrils. The gloves of my tired arms peeled away to new limbs of chestnut brown with willowy hands and fingernails like dogwood petals. Flaying the torso was painful, but how proud I was of my high round breasts, my belly rippling where it met the pelt reaching up to my waist. *You sexy fuck*, I whispered to the creature in my bathroom mirror, then grabbed each ear and pulled upwards. A lake of hair fell over my shoulder and down to my navel. My eyes were ringed with black paint, my mouth, cleft as a hare. This was no dream, I tell you; this was just the beginning. In my zeal I trod on my tail three times before draping it over my arm and, grabbing my best bag and throwing in the knives, I was off to where the wild ones go to dance among the boabs.

The Ologist's Ego, Conquered

He said he'd snuck out for the night, he'd recently separated
from the pre-frontal cortex of a doctor
and what did I think of *that*?

He wouldn't be drawn on the specialty
but it had to be an *ologist* of sorts —
there was something of the teenager

about his forearms, pale and smooth,
his hands with their close-clipped fingernails
that foretold microsurgery.

While the doctor slept, tucked up with his trophy wife,
his ego had slipped from the house and I found myself
next to him at 4 a.m. in the garden bar.

You like my scrubs? he asked with a flourish —
cocky bastard — and all the while I was thinking
they'd look better around his knees.

But I said nothing and necked my tequila,
licked the salt off the back of my hand,
flicked my tail at a moth.

It occurs to me now that my guilt was misplaced —
I was on borrowed time myself.
This would be no ordinary courtship.

Reader, we needed no line of coke,
no champagne fountain; it was going to happen
and it was simply a matter of where.

A peacock screamed from the topiary.
The best thing about a pelt, I discovered,
as distinct from a frock or skinny jeans,

is the freedom it affords shenanigans.
This was hardly making love,
but a savage mating among mock orange and fig.

Damn him, he was good and he knew it;
Navy-SEAL discipline and a few tricks
up his pale-blue baggy sleeve.

The stars had faded from the eastern sky
by the time he anointed me, wiping his bristled chin
across my high breasts, taut belly and furred thighs.

A trickle of blood tattooed his shoulder. His lip
was swollen where I'd silenced his bragging.
We panted as pink dawn backlit the canopy.

I didn't like it — my knees would ache for days —
but who says it's supposed to be fun anyway?
I kicked him off and made my way back to the bar.

Mother Creature

DAMSELFLY

Age thirteen, skin splits down her body.
She emerges, clad in shimmer, all sequin
and wing-glass. Pretty head thrown back, clasped
by mate after mate. Green river air: shantung
scribbled with their heart-shaped pen.

SALMON

Seaward, she's drawn tail-first. A river,
that silversmith, arming her, scale by scale.
The ocean has no boundary, save memory.
Though her flesh corals with experience
she'll dodge cane rod, vernal bear,
and return to the gravel of the smolt.

PELICAN

Grotesque pink bill pressed to her quilled
leather corset releases the last minnow
from gular folds. If they want
to believe she pierces her bosom
to blood-nourish her young, let them.

VIXEN

Bring on the night! Let her skulk
and cry, dog-fox by her side,
blackberry picking in fur coat and heels.
By dawn she's back to earth, her cubs
an auburn ball. The sick one she'll carry
to the wood's edge and dump it. Just in case.

PILOT WHALE

Her skin-rubber, hashed and scored
with scars, hides an armchair heart.
Her glands can still suckle a youngster
bored by waiting for his mother.
Her children's children will be doctors.

Chrysalis

Day one you are tiny and serious —
peach-downy head umami-scented,
thighs, plump and creased

as croissants. In a week they'll split
your warm puppy belly, spill your innards
on the stainless steel,

untwist your tangled bowel.
Afterwards, a centipede scar will hide
under a candy-striped blanket

wrapping you like a lozenge.
By age four you'll have survived
several swipes on your life, emerging

bold and lively from the pupa.
All this I don't yet know, as I stand,
pear-heavy, by the Perspex crib.

They scan your brain, looking
for the missing part, but it's there.
The fools. Of course it's there.

A doctor once sat opposite us at a teak desk.
With babies, we told him,
you take them when you can get them.
What do you mean, what do we want to do?

Naming the First-born

You are as I dreamt you,
alert and serene, packed like glass
in peach skin, watching blue
and green flash past the car.
Your name shall be Ashling.

Your eyes map my face
(eye-nose-lips), two cocoa beans,
a throwback to a stray Armada gene
from scuttled Spanish ships.
We shall name you Valentina.

Your road here was violent;
nurses weigh my dressings
to chart blood loss, heavy
blankets hide a battlefield.
You shall be called Athena.

You discover me like a lover,
skin to skin, mouth to nipple,
foot soles to lips,
marbled belly to my kiss.
Your name shall be Alaïa.

Your fingers sway, anemones.
You are ancient as ferns,
fiddleheads unspooled in shade.
I watch your willow hands all day.
My child, your name is Grace.

My Son at Bedtime

after Jericho Brown

That time of day he doesn't need to try.
Attention is the opposite of dream.

> You mustn't pay attention to your dreams:
> his Manga figures have no nostrils, see?

You figure that his angry nostrils bleed
because, beyond your kisses, knots amass;

> he's beyond kisses, but not beyond caress —
> and cannot read the letters in the book

but likes the letters traced across his back.
His scapulae protrude just as your own

> spectacularly bloom. But he has grown
> since your lap was his favourite chair. These days

you read his favourite armchair travel tales
at night, so he no longer has to try.

Motel Ghosts

Ever wonder where they go? The souls
of the extinct — not the bones
of pipistrelles, finer than eyelashes,
the rufous down of boobook owls
or starry pelts of quolls,
but the imprint of their lives on time's roll.
I've seen them in the toile-covered walls
of dim motel rooms,
their faces spooking restless guests.
Or on a stuffy sofa,
patterned by day with swollen roses,
there, night-time mouths appear
as clownish leers or Munchian howls
and Rorschach ink-blot bats
that twitch their leather folds.
In the chintz gap, the Antipodean
face of the moon is a fur-seal pup
and only if you look aslant at the blankest gap,
will they appear — a spray of gems
atumble on a velvet tray.
Look too close and they evanesce
like the Slipper Orchid's flutes
known only to a blasé damselfly.
This quiet menagerie of lost ones
wanders the quarter light mouthing: *Remember us.*

The Irish for Yes

after Ciaran Carson

There is no Irish word for *yes*.
On Inisheer upturned currachs stud the sand
like stranded humpback calves.

Cumulus embellishes the sea,
egg-white whipped to stiff meringue
inside the sky's green bowl.

Fishing flounder — easy if you're in the know:
a foot of catgut tied below the weight,
a hook to line the seabed where they hide.

But I am not a tomboy anymore. Not game
to handle ragworm bait, I ask the man
in oilskins if he can do the dirty work.

He says *I can*. His Aran sweater's ribbed
with blocks of honeycomb I want to stroke.
The sea turns navy blue.

After, I'll send letters penned on onionskin
but if he writes to me *I will, I do*,
I'll never get the note.

When my mother taught me how to knit
I practised until I could turn out blackberry
and trellis in my sleep.

She also taught me how to debone lemon sole:
split the flesh along the spine,
lift the lattice bone.

I ask the skipper if I might steal a kiss.
He says *you may*. His lips are salted as a pretzel
and when I open my eyes again the sea is turquoise.

Grey Man

Good name for you, I think at first — 'grey man',
grey hair — once thickly black, now thinly wan.
Steel eyes, your teeth off-kilter, off-white,
and those grey eyebrows — very strange, quite

fascinating. You say fuck the norm,
then we talk of love and Leonard Cohen.
You bring up 'Chelsea Hotel #2';
your cheek is pink, your thoughts are kinda blue.

I rise (adroit) and close the office door
so *they* don't hear, and then we talk of more
love songs; your eyes abruptly change their hue
as oceans change when sunlight pierces through.

Your gaze is on my back while I make tea.
Which one were you again? you shyly tease.
Which screen goddess, unsaid, but clearly there
above the boiling kettle. My pupils flare

and from the corner of my eye I see
a spectrum where your ashen form had been —
the sun refracted through my window pane.
I turn and stare but all is colourless, plain,

yet as I turn I sense it there —
a rainbow on my ergonomic chair.
The penny drops; that's not the goddamned sea!
It's your true colours shown to me.

And through the fissures of your loosened skin
a catalogue of blue flickers within.
Your moniker describes you errantly —
they should have named you for the sea.

Lockdown Boogie

Let's go dancing — in our heads.
You take my hand, I toss the rose.
We mustn't kiss, we both agree
that would be irresponsible.
Can you hear that slide guitar?
Or is it cellos and a mandolin?
But certainly the blues. We've waded
through discarded masks
like leaf-litter in the alley
and stumbled down the stairway
to the Blind Tiger in our minds.
The barman ties his paisley scarf
like a highwayman's disguise,
while he mixes your Negroni
and concocts, in purple,
his signature Amelia Earhart,
dipping the rim of the glass
first in egg white, then fine sugar.
You whisper of a masked ball
between the wars, a faceless, silent party;
how they wove their spells — the contour
where velvet meets throat,
the barest brush of lace,
and, despite our best intentions,
your mouth works its way up my arm
which in turn tastes your lips
and when you reach my neck
I tilt my head. And, reader,
you don't know if *towards* or *away*
but will just have to imagine.

The Important Things

i.m. Marianne Ihlen

There's a word in Scots Gaelic — *sgrìob* —
which refers to the tingle on the upper lip
just before you take a sip of whisky.
We are talking — after the burial,
now they've allowed funerals again —
across a table no bigger than a dinner plate
about those we've lost to the virus,
and *whisky* or *whiskey* — the important things —
when Roy Buchanan comes on the jukebox
and I can almost taste the light
film of sweat on your skin.
I should have known it right then:
an inventor will always be curious,
and that here, in this bar, months from now,
you will sit in false darkness
with another muse,
while on our white-board veranda,
its double swing written by Harper Lee,
I'll dip my best bristle brush
in tin after tin of green —
viridian, sap, olive, emerald —
and slap paint mixed with salt onto timber shades
until every trace of off-white is erased.
I'll forgive you, in time, everything
but the way you changed my name
in the song that made you famous,
trimming a syllable to rhyme with *began*;
the irony of that, since it was the end,
and not even our story,
though all unhappy stories resemble each other.
But let's not catastrophize,
we haven't yet begun, and right here, right now,
in The Fiddler's Arms,

there's a feeling coming over me,
a surface tension close to my upper lip,
that no English word can describe.

Skin Symphony

They are there if you listen.
On the train, in the Laundromat —
the instruments, I mean:
bells, stirring in two-way stretch cotton
(their owner slumped in the window seat,
his work boots tapping a secret rhythm),
timpani buttoned under a cashier's blouse,
a cello bound by polyester pinafore
in salmon pink. She thinks
the air is flecked with soap dust,
doesn't realize it's rosin from her bow.
Air flows through apertures
where, later, fingers will flutter,
strings blur under the rub of horsehair,
their discordant mewl barely heard
above the swish of the train,
the hum of machine,
louder in the darkness of tunnel
or the lull of rinse cycle, then soft again.
Tuning up, they're getting ready
for this evening's symphony
of skin to begin at precisely 10.15.

⌒

And you can never explain it in physical terms —
what happens between two people
on an ordinary bed, in an ordinary room.
Let me ask, could you school the cuttlefish
in Ludwig's *Emperor* (second movement)
in terms of anvil, hammer and stirrup?
Paint the hues of daybreak for the mole?
There is only air, compressed and stretched.
There is always space between skins,
no matter how close they press.

No touch, only music —
an oboe sings, a cello answers.
Locked within the strands of collagen,
atoms built of smaller blocks,
each one a capsule packed with strings,
each string a note that's yet to play.

⌣

Afterwards, they lie curled,
two bass clefs facing this way, that.
They talk of anything, of childhood,
and croak the lyrics of Paul Simon songs,
this, the highlight,
now the players have left the stage.
Sleep will come later, a raft
pushed out on a starred sea.
What oak bed? Which room?
There is nothing here
but phosphorescence
undulating on their border.
Only this small stage
drifting on the night swell,
a single baton on its floor.

A Gradual Eden

After the lava had cooled,
hardened like a carapace
on the graves of our marriages,
nothing happened for a while.
Sure, you and I still talked all night,
once dared to walk arm-in-arm
like a real couple
to the Vietnamese restaurant
with the string-bead curtain
and the napkins folded into swans.
I had to learn the basics:
I only knew your thoughts,
but not, for instance,
how you took your coffee,
how you swam at five each morning,
leaving me to wake alone.
Nothing grew on the hard-baked basalt
of *us*. Ditches that defined
our lanes and highways vanished,
once-shady trees now jutted like antlers
where the lightning had struck them.
When the strawberries were gone
we ate dandelion and fiddlehead ferns.
You were inventive in the kitchen,
but I was sick of roots and leaves; I wanted
Passiflora (or violets at the very least).
Once, longing for old comforts, you peeked
back under the edge of the rock-crust
for a glimpse of green, but the lawns
were mustard and thistle-pocked.
Twice I peeked too.
Watering didn't help much.
Neither did planting seeds.
After a year or two we got used to it.
Gave up trying.

Hung up boots.
One day we saw the rock was dusted
with faintest green, just a bristle,
like your beard at 5 a.m. — no more.
And then we saw a stem unfurl,
and then the flowers came.

Sold a Pup

i.m. Anthony Minghella

I envied Kristin Scott Thomas, emerging from the biplane,
shaking out the halo of her mane; her slim silhouette

against the Cairo night sky; making love in a church
cloakroom while, outside, ladies ate mince pies. I liked her

best reflected in his convex eye, *I can still taste you.*
Yes, this, what they talk of when they talk of love.

Funny, how you never shot her with a social worker,
nibbling a stale wafer as they rehash it one more time,

or, heart in mouth, crushing another cockroach
with her shoe in a neat one-bedder, handy to everything.

Oh, Anthony, if I ever get you on your own in a cobble-
stone alley there'll be hell to pay, my darling. Now I am carried,

dying, into the clinic, and you don't even spy the thimble
around my neck, the one you picked up in the bazaar.

Why must you persist in wearing your heart on your sleeve?
you ask. *You idiot, I always wear it. I've always worn it.*

I've always loved you.

Forty-four

A champagne hangover is no way to start the new year,
not when the mercury reaches forty-four and we are draped
like wax over the arms of leather lounges, trying
to suck the cool out of anything shiny.

My tangerine sherbet cotton dress has darkened in a delta
down my back and clings to my thighs as I rinse cherries,
slice the shocked cheeks off mangoes, criss-cross them
and turn them inside out. My brain feels like this.

I hand over the keys of my Fiat Bambino to the guests,
who can't resist driving to Bondi. It seemed like a good idea
the night before, as we all crammed in after the fireworks.
Sure this car's a grand yoke, Niall, from the back,

plastic glass in one hand, youngest daughter bundled
in the boot like a hostage. Today they're not so sure.
The car's flimsy fan is not helping. Eileen, between
two daughters, declares that Veuve really is overrated.

We pick like gluttons at the fruit on the platter, query
why cherries are not cherry-flavoured. My makeup slides
on a film of sweat. This was the summer before we installed
the air-con we wouldn't need again for seven years.

The bathers are back, panting, shoulders rashered; no one
gallivants today. Eileen fills a bowl with iced water
and we take turns cooling our feet. Outside cicadas scream.
Niall plays a chord on the guitar. *Is it too early for Mojitos?*

Poaching Stone Fruit on the Long Weekend

A small, one-chef kitchen.
He wears sudsy cuffs, twirls taps.
I split ripe peaches and dark plums
and drop them in a pan of sugar-syrup
with a cigarillo cinnamon quill.
Vanilla pods probe my appetite like question marks.
He brushes past to collect
the breakfast things, sweeps
eggshell and bacon rind into the bin.
The peaches loosen in their skins,
plums fizz at a simmer.
My side-opening dress has riddled
his fingers into words:
What's the point of a zip
where my hands can't reach anything?
We pinball off the Caesarstone.
We taste of Fairy liquid
and fermenting juice.
Too old for kitchen bench
or table top, the marble tiles too hard,
we argue the toss:
You like being on top?
I do; you look like a boy.
I am a boy.
The stone fruit comes on to the boil
and the air is thick with nectar.
Sweet liquids spurt from the pan.

What I Learned from the Dentist

Clifford has very white teeth, which I find reassuring, as I lie, belly up, in his chair. He talks all the time as he works. David Attenborough projected on the ceiling is silent, so Clifford is voiceover for the murder of a Thomson's gazelle or the hatching of a baby Cayman.

～

Hue is not the same as value. Clifford holds a series of teeth close to my own, each Vita Classic shade atop a metal rod, like a lollipop or impaled head. There are twenty-nine shades of white, he tells me, more than Inuit words for snow. He is deciding between 'grey' and 'reddish-grey' for the hue of my new crown. I'm unsettled but I calm at the sight of his incisors, so close to my eye that I can see their faint ridges, worn almost smooth. There is more to it than shade, he says, there is also *chroma* — the strength of colour. The tooth is not defined by hue alone, he says, but by its story — the tearing, the grinding. And the smiling.

～

The smiling dentist, they call him. He beams from his shingle and business card, famous for his pain-free dentistry, which is why I traverse eight suburbs by train. Sometimes I fall asleep in his chair during root canal, sometimes on my way home, off my face on Valium, my forehead rattling against the double glaze.

～

Home is where the heart is, Elvis drifts in from reception. Clifford's lived here all his life. His parents emigrated in the '60s when Mao was changing red from *stop* to *go*. He asks me lots of questions: Why did you move so far away? Will you ever move home? Home is here, I say, with my children and my man. A new sky and trees. He says only a child can know a tree — its seeds and blossoms, the texture of its skin. We are alike, he says. In cities the world over, for every Chinese restaurant there is an Irish pub. Why no Irish restaurants? I say, why no Chinese pubs? He laughs and utters a word I don't understand to Joy. She aspirates my spit. The tube grabs the words from my tongue.

~

Sometimes (I tell Clifford) when I'm ensconced in a smoky snug in a seaboard town where people still speak Irish with the *blas* — which means 'taste' or 'flavour' as well as 'accent' — I bring all five fingertips together to my lips and close my eyes. I feel the language stirring in my tongue, old knowledge passed down like a fear of snakes. When I hear it spoken — the poetry of it — I register meaning only slowly, like a snippet of the shipping forecast for Irish coastal waters — *Belmullet, West-Southwest, Cloudy, 8 miles, 1015, Steady*. My tongue was stamped out, I tell him, like a spot fire. A few embers still smoulder but there is nothing left to catch.

~

Clifford says the world is full of the dispossessed. *So many people now*. I tell him how the Poles came to Ireland, when there was work for a while, how they flocked to the outpost of a continent, looking for riches. They were so poor they ate the swans, leaving nothing but a smattering of feathers on the banks of the canal.

─

I see colours, I tell Clifford one day, under the effect of laughing gas. The colours are not from the gas, but the confession is — I have never told anyone that each day of the week has its own hue. Bingo, he says. But our colours don't match, apart from Monday, which is pigeon-grey. His are uniform, like the muted puce of Tuesday; mine, variegated — the Brussels-sprout green of Friday. He says Yevgeny Zamati also had chromestesia, where words evoke colours, but I don't know who he means. Zamati also had to emigrate, he says. I say I didn't have to leave, though people used to think that when I first came to Australia — a Catholic girl with a Protestant beau.

─

Clifford types up his notes and I tell him how a friend in Ireland has been haunted by the word *noirish*, used to describe a certain kind of writing. All he could see was 'No Irish' staked in his uncle's garden when he set up home in the US in the '50s. 'Then Kennedy got elected,' he told me, 'and that shut them up.' Clifford says the Chinese were also hated. *No one who can rise before the sun each day of the year will fail to make his family rich.* I tell him how we scattered like the spores of late potato blight during the Great Hunger — on coffin ships and, later, J-1 visas. We built roads and railways, waited tables. Drunks and poets. In cramped kitchens, late at night, we sang about what every Paddy wants: *Fad saol agat, gob fliuch agus bás in Éirinn* — Long life, a wet mouth and death in Ireland.

─

Before I leave, Joy hands me a shiny bag: travel-size toothpaste, extra-soft brush, a tube of bleaching gel promising a 'Whiter. Brighter. You.' Clifford waves, Joy waves and, next door, in the window of The Golden Lotus, the fortune cat waves too.

Curracloe Revisited

July 2016

Only last week we walked here, raincoats
throat-zipped, scarfs doubled,
a seal our sole companion.

The sand, a shade between cement
and cardboard, released fine powder,
whipped our ankles.

Two horses thundered past.
You *swam* here? he said, and made me
wonder if time had distorted it all,

if the flipbooks were real.
Did I really, age nine and nut-brown,
fossick for pretty shells,

eat hard-boiled eggs
and scallions, drink Tupperware-tea
after my third dip of the day?

Today he has left for Moscow,
but I have my answer: the sky —
kite-ribboned, Falcon-brochure blue.

Hoards throng in every shade
of sunburn, white and bottle-tan.
Mothers — ankle deep — hike skirts,

mark toddlers. Candy-striped
windbreakers stake out territory
keeping sand off lubed backs

and lacquered boobs.
Installed on deckchairs, leeward,
women cluck and sizzle,

Sure this is better than Spain,
talk of the best swimsuit
for an even tan, the antics of kids,

husbands, the important things.
My youngest, lithe in triangle
bikini, trawls the littoral zone

for tiny clams in mauves
and peachy pinks, each
with a pinhole

at the apex, perfect for a necklace.
The road tar has melted on the way
back to cars parked in ditches.

Outside the games' arcade,
teens eye each other off
as practice material; it could be

Curracloe Beach 1986,
the year we dredged the sea
for our parish priest. Or, for that matter,

Rush Beach 1976, cars
in a prairie-wagon ring,
jelly-fish brandished at terry-

towelled girls and a sun-worshipper,
caught off guard in a cross-
your-heart bra.

The seal has fled to warmer waters,
like my love, who believes all this
was invented by a woman far from home.

Unfinished

Moscow Station, St Petersburg

At the café you have coffee and blinchiki, and I, tea
    and smoked salmon, discs of pink grapefruit.

Well, here we are, you say, and I say, yes, here we are. We make
    a list of must-sees — you: Peter and Paul Fortress;

me: Pushkin's apartment, Fabergé. We both choose the Hermitage,
    and you say we are building our narrative.

I pull out *Eugene Onegin*; you pronounce it like a Russian,
    and we laugh, call for more tea and coffee, talk some more

and you ask if I ever finished *Anna Karenina* that time,
    years ago now. No, I say. I was too afraid to discover

what happens when a woman does this; I didn't read the end,
    oblivious to the danger of a man, or a train.

Anna Karenina Smiles as She Steps off the Platform

after Guy Goffette

Admit it, woman, to die not having lived is common.
　　Who would trudge the poplar-lined avenue to where

it meets Moral High Ground? Who would not have gold
　　fleck her eyes, who wouldn't lunge into her bodice

and produce a shining meaty heart for all to look upon
　　in curiosity? You chose to coat your daily bread

in butter, thick and yellow, chose Passiflora over
　　cabbage rose or chamomile. This path is narrow,

vine-choked, but runs true as the aorta. They say
　　a woman only has so many heartbeats in her life

and yours are running low. You will have a sudden death —
　　savage (yes!) as all best endings are, blood

returned to iron. Know you can hold your lovely head
　　high in the station lamplight. Know you tried.

PART TWO

No one knocks any longer to ask
how she likes her new house
or how she has arranged her sweet furniture.
— Bernard O'Donoghue
('The Move', from the Middle English)

Charmed

On special nights, in winter, my mother wears
    a tight-sleeved dress in emerald, under fur.

She lifts my fringe to kiss me and sings a tune
    her mother sang to her: *Go to sleep, my baby,*

close your pretty eyes, but I don't close them. I want
    to lose my fingers in mink, inhale the arctic scent

of her perfume and, most of all, I want to listen
    to the tinkle of her charms. Sometimes she twists

the bracelet in the night-light's glow, shows
    me the golden scorpion, her honeymoon Jersey cow,

the jet plane charm they gifted her
    the day she left Aer Lingus to have me.

My favourites hide secrets: the tiny church that hinges
    open to reveal a bride and groom; a lion

inside a wheeled cage; a disc of gold you flick
    with a fingernail to read Happy Birthday.

This will be yours one day, she says, and tucks
    the candlewick to stop me rolling out

and then she's gone. There's only Holly Hobbie
    staring down from wallpaper at a child

who doesn't understand that when the bracelet is hers
    the charm will be broken.

Flowering Cherry

A tree can sell a house, the agent says,
when they view 10 Beech Drive as newlyweds.
Its shot-silk trunk stands so close to the hedge
its blossom carpet-bombs the street by May.
Come June, it casts lemonade shade as tar-
seams melt, stick to bare feet kicking cans
or skipping ropes slung between the footpaths,
grounded only for a passing car.
September's red and ochre pot-pourri
of leaves will bank against the windowsills.
Boughs that vein the sky in winter will
be knobbed with sticky buds again by spring.
Four years my young mother sees it bloom
before my bud unfurls, pink, in her womb.

Debutante Dress

Most of the girls choose pastel satin with '80s puff sleeves. We'll find it, you say, and we leaf through a book of patterns, choosing tartan taffeta gathered to a fitted bodice of black velvet with boat neck and full-length sleeve. I may have seen one like it in a Hitchcock flick or *Elle* magazine. I stand, stiff-armed, in the kitchen, craning to see the portable TV, while you nudge my chin, chalk up gores for my linear figure, your mouth full of pins. The sewing box between us is a treasure chest: pincushions in cadmium red, copper pinking shears, loose rolls of rick-rack and broderie anglaise, and all to your humming — distant whale song over the Singer's growl, the bobbin's whirr. I get it now, Mother; sixteen is too young to be wandering around on a school night looking for a place to stay even if I really *did* have a row with my best friend, even if I *did* sleep in the guest room of my boyfriend's house while his big sister kept vigil all night, apart from one phone call to a woman, up late, gathering taffeta into a black bodice. It's that sullen age, when threats of curfews and docked pocket money are discarded like parkas in the hall. *I'm not finishing your dress* ... It's less than a week to the ball. You hold out for a couple of days. I mean you *cannot* abandon it. We both know it's a knockout.

Like Double Denim

I must call my mother,
tell her about the lilies, hibiscus
and fan palms on my swimsuit,

how it looks like a holiday,
and how the salesgirl's eyes
glanced off my small breasts

and chose this suit
from a large display, saying,
This will complement your figure.

In the changing room, a kimono.
When I asked for my size, she said,
That's from the same story.

So now I'm wearing them together,
the whole story,
poolside in the resort

I know my mother would love:
blue cocktails, lychee perfume,
guitar on the breeze.

She'll close her eyes,
tilt her head, ask about
pattern and cut.

In our separate hemispheres
we'll defer to Winsor & Newton —
Cobalt and Turquoise

overlaid with Permanent Green,
blossoms of Scarlet Lake,
Burnt Umber stamens.

I must call.
If Dad's in the garden
I'll get her voicemail:

I'm unable to come
to the phone right now.
Leave your flowers after the tone.

Mother, I Am Your Mother Now

We first talked under water, through quiet peristalsis.

I don't recall the words you spoke
    but I know they meant: At last. You are here.

I never told you I was jellyfish,
    velvet worm, nautilus, before I came to you.

I'll drift the length of my umbilicus,
    a coracle of skin on bone.

I'll feel your pulse again, ripple through amnion
    where my limb buds wave your rhythm.

My words will cross this liquor sea,
    wash up on the cobalt shores of your inner ear.

I'll carry you inside, as you once carried me.

Uprooted

She missed the warning signs —
the weekends in the boondocks,
his liver-and-white gun-dog pup.

She packed our woollens up
in tea chests for the transfer
far from her brothers and their wives.

Damp ran down the kitchen walls
until my father had them
dry-lined and papered with tea roses.

All day my mother heard the hum
of telegraph wires, distant sheep,
a solitary bee.

She'd yet to learn a clump of primrose
should be left to charm
the shadows of a dry-stone wall,

not planted into baskets lined with moss.
The chests were stacked in outhouses
for season after season,

ragged plywood snagging at your arm.
And this is how, a child learns,
precious things are stored.

His Hybrid Tea Roses

from my mother's garden diary 1975

Piccadilly
  sunrise in each pointed bloom

Fragrant Cloud
  scarlet petals soaked in glass

Duke of Windsor
  a love story in blood-orange

Pharaoh
  perfume lingering in the Austin

Rose Guajard
  on a corsage, at the races

Ena Harkness
  my bleeding heart

She Loved

after Anna Akhmatova

gingham and polka dots, not just on napkins —
　　in ruffles on swimsuits or piped round a plate;

hats in great boxes like candy-striped cheeses,
　　her favourite a trilby bought with my first pay;

Tupperware storage in delicate hues,
　　with curlicue labels for sago and arrowroot;

salmon for breakfast when staying at hotels
　　or cooked by my father, who could be hard to love;

chocolate, just a square, or a nibble of yours
　　or a mini-Flake stashed in an old mantel clock;

a night at the opera — especially Puccini —
　　and a late supper of *moules* and Sauv Blanc;

bridge tips she snipped from *The Irish Times*
　　and practising them over nightcaps with Dad;

and the signature theme from 'The Onedin Line'
　　she said would be played at her funeral mass.

The Space Between

Mother, your wig may fool your brothers
but I know your wayward hair, like my own,
wouldn't stay in shape like this;

I know there's a slim, curved space between
your scalp and the fine, silk netting,
right at your crown;

I know you admire the fuller shape of your head
though you'd never have wished for it all those years
if you'd known this was how you'd get it.

Some nights I dream I roam that airless field,
running my hands through sparse hair
like moonlit wheat.

Running Out

You're home for our whole trip,
can't stop looking at Grace —
her wispy hair, farmer's walk,

the way her insteps bulge
like mushrooms over Mary Janes.
You read the story of a queen

who longs for children
as Grace runs her hands
over gifts under the tree.

We make short outings,
long shadows in the garden,
as you wind wool for the pompom

of the sugar-pink hat you're knitting.
Camouflaged on the faded couch,
you put down the wool to rub

shea butter into hands too small
for their skin, say you can't wait
to be in Sydney heat again.

A list of reasons I mustn't stay —
and, anyway, you won't be home again
from hospital for months.

We talk of remission; how you'll be over
to see the baby once you're better.
We almost fool each other.

You wind the wool until it runs out,
tie a double knot and snip around the edge.
A flurry of pink snow floats in the air

as you trim a ball that's not as full
as you'd like and say,
There is never enough.

Going Home

Our last day in Wexford,
in January pre-dawn,
I stand in the hall

where your paintings
of two birds
hang on the wall.

You're wearing your wig
and, over your nightie,
a hand-knit cardigan —

indigo mohair,
with a band of cerise and lime,
like the northern lights.

When I hug you —
bird-small now,
yet still so vast in my life —

it could be our last embrace.
You grow warm in my arms
until car doors call time.

Driving north to Dublin,
I see, on the horizon,
a streak of pink and green.

I watch it flicker, gutter and die.

Confetti

The news comes on Grace's second birthday.
Mam's in trouble, Dad's voice on the phone,
with the tone of a cyclone warning.

As I assemble a retro toy kitchen
I plot how I will trick the airline
about my due date and go to you.

But the surgeon is firm,
fires words like *shock* and *sudden labour*.
We talk on the phone a lot. You say,

I don't think I have much time, and tell me
how the nurses say you should go home,
how your nieces come to visit,

how you love the view of Dublin.
I write my last letter to you —
all the things I want to say,

the things I *get*, now I'm a mother.
A week later, when I make my daily call,
you hear my ring-tone, try to sit.

They calm you but you want to speak
so they press the small sponge to your lips
so you can tell me — through your morphine haze —

that my letter arrived that morning,
they've read it to you, over and over,
and each time you feel as though you're covered in roses.

False Memory

My sister is under strict instructions
to relay every detail so I can remember
as if I'm there, instead of here,

wandering Sydney's Lower North Shore
with a toddler in a pram: the May morning
in St Brigid's church, the coffin

where my mother lies *resplendent*
in the fuchsia suit she wore to my wedding,
her better-than-her-own-hair wig,

blue eyes closed, lips shaped to a smile —
she was always smiling — but also closed,
no straight white teeth grazed with Rimmel.

I clearly recall the hymns,
hummed to myself for years afterwards,
in the shower or while vacuuming — different

from what she'd wanted at her funeral.
The choir, not up to Khachaturian's
'Theme from Spartacus',

sings 'Going Home'. And the flowers!
Irises, of course, and the wreath
that goes into the ground with her —

a small wreath of zinc-white roses
I never saw
but distinctly recall.

Pink for a Boy

The baby comes on cue, as in a romantic comedy, with mild contractions starting in the small hours and pain building up to 8 — the book says 8 means head for hospital — then stalling to nothing as soon as we reach the ward. Stage fright. The nurse says the key to a good enema is *high, hot and a hell of a lot* and I'm back to 8 within minutes. In the shower, my hands pressed high on the tiles, I stamp and count for hours until my blood pressure drops so low I slide down the wall and pass out. I can still hear: the squeak of rubber sole on polished floor, the rustle of newspapers as my husband is alerted. I know my child's spine and mine are grinding off each other with every squeeze and I should be on all fours, but they put me on my back, helpless as a beetle in a schoolyard, and wait for my blood pressure to rise so they can give me the good drugs. The anaesthetist is the most attractive man I've ever seen and I now understand why junkies fall in love with their dealers. The child is suctioned out by the forehead — bruised, blue-grey, still. The habitually-smooth obstetrician barks at my husband to snip the cord — such a small word, *snip*, for a huge thing — and then runs, he runs, with the child held in front like a boiled chicken to a high table where nurses swarm with tubes and monitors and stainless steel to startle him to life. And the world slows. A drop of blood is suspended midway between gurney and tile. There's only a sea of scrubs and hairnets crowded around an altar where a child farewells his undersea life and pinks up. *A boy*, the doc says, *aren't you clever*, as if this were my doing, and he looks at me with his hard, blue eyes that say, *you see now, what would have happened if the shock brought it on?* And so, Mother, you have a grandson. You, who longed for a big family of sons and had to make do with two girls — a perfect, pinked-up, rose-madder boy.

Salt Rain, Wexford

As soon as they let me travel with the baby
I take the long-haul via Abu Dhabi
and arrive in Dublin on your birthday.

Dad collects us and I see that ageing
is not linear; this last year he's caught up
on ten years of looking the same.

He talks all the way to Blackwater,
like a man who hasn't spoken in months.
At the edge of the village we see the church

and I ask to stop. He shows me where you are,
in a new part of the cemetery,
your grave unpretentious but tasteful,

as you were. No photo on yours,
unlike the teenagers' graves that flank it,
their high-school faces witness

a jet-lagged woman talking to polished granite
while an infant kicks in his stroller.
The cut flowers are dying but there

are glazed black planters full of blooms.
And I show you why. I unclick the child
from his seat and hold him to the sky.

But you say nothing. I had pictured
a backdrop of light rain — the kind
that doesn't clear the weather —

but there's just the muffle of low cloud.
It's only later, over the skeleton of lemon sole
on a Denby plate, that rain finally arrives.

Notes

page 14 This poem contains a quote from 'Psychological charac-
teristics associated with tobacco smoking behaviour'
(Rondina et al, J. bras. pneumol. vol.33 no.5 São Paulo,
Sept/Oct 2007).

page 24 'The Courser's Tale' reflects on the plight of the 6,000
greyhounds killed each year in Ireland for being 'too
slow' (*RTÉ Investigates: Greyhounds, Running for Their
Lives*, June 2019) and was inspired by an image by an
unknown artist (circa 1880) in Getty Open Content
Program in the *Visual Verse*: Anthology of Art and
Words (2020).

page 32 For the form of this poem see Jericho Brown's 'Duplex'.

page 34 See Ciaran Carson's poem 'The Irish for No'.

page 38 This poem alludes to a response from Marianne Ihlen
when asked what she thought of Leonard Cohen's song
'So Long, Marianne'.

page 44 Words in italics are from *The English Patient* by Michael
Ondaatje. The third stanza riffs off *What We Talk About
When We Talk About Love* by Raymond Carver.

page 47 This quotes a traditional Chinese proverb, 'No one who
can rise before the sun each day of the year will fail to
make his family rich' and includes a line from a conver-
sation with Jim McElroy, 'Then Kennedy got elected.
And that shut them up', used with his kind permission.

page 55 The opening line was prompted by Guy Goffette's poem,
'Letter to the Unknown Woman Across the Street III'.

page 59 'Charmed' includes a line from the song 'Go to Sleep,
My Baby' (originally titled 'The Wyoming Lullaby'),
written by the American composer, Gene Williams,
aka Lawrence Wright.

page 66 This was inspired by a list of roses discovered in my
mother's diary.

page 67 See Anna Akhmatova's untitled poem beginning 'He
loved three things alone'.

Acknowledgements

Acknowledgements are due to the editors of the following publications where some of these poems, or versions of them, were published first: *The Australian, Banshee, The Blue Nib, Bold+Italic, Headstuff, Irises: The University of Canberra Vice-Chancellor's International Poetry Prize* (2017), *The Irish Times, Live Encounters, Magma Poetry, Meanjin, Mslexia, Newcastle Poetry Prize Anthology* (2019, 2020), *Orbis Literary Journal, Poems from Pandemia* (Southword Editions), *Poetry d'Amour Anthology, Poetry Ireland Review, Rascal, ROPES, Southword, The Tangerine, Verity La* and *Visual Verse*.

Nine of these poems were published in *Satyress* (Southword Editions, 2020).

A version of 'Salt Rain, Wexford' won *An Post* Irish Book Awards (APIBA) Poem of the Year, 2019. 'On Reaching 45 the Poet Realizes She Is Only 23' won the Aesthetica Creative Writing Award, 2019. 'Grey Man' won the Poetry d'Amour Contest, 2017.

I acknowledge gratefully the Arts Council/An Chomhairle Ealaíon for a bursary in Literature.

Sincere thanks to Peter Fallon and the team at The Gallery Press for their support and patience in editing and producing this book.

I would like to thank Martina Evans who selected my work for the Hennessy Emerging Poetry Award (2019). Thanks also to my early manuscript readers Maeve Valentine and Gary Valentine. I'm sincerely grateful to the following people who gave their time and energy to earlier drafts of these poems: Anthony Lawrence, Kevin Higgins, the poets in my writing group Poets Abroad (including Ricky, Jo, Morag, Barbara, Bobbie, Fran and Geoff) and my colleagues from the 2019 Poetry Ireland Introductions Series and the 2020 Varuna Residential Fellowship.

I would not be writing these words were it not for the following people: my parents, Tom and Iris, who filled our house with books and fostered my creativity; my kind, funny and wonderful children, Grace, Harry and Emily, who share me with the muse; and Graeme, the Grey Man himself, whose presence in my life has made this book — and many other things — possible.